Write to Know Series

Middle School

S0-BFA-536

Nonfiction Writing Prompts for

Science

- Anne M. Holbrook, M.Ed.
- Rosemary Ruthven, M.S., Literacy Specialist
- Edited by Amy M. Whited, M.A.

ALP
Advanced
Learning
Press

A L P
Advanced
Learning
Press

Advanced Learning Press
317 Inverness Way South, Suite 150
Englewood, CO 80112
Phone (800) 844-6599 or (303) 504-9312 ∎ Fax (303) 504-9417
www.MakingStandardsWork.com/Advanced_Learning_Press.html

ISBN: 1-933196-13-0

Printed in the United States of America

10 09 08 07 06 05   01 02 03 04 05 06 07 08 09

CONTENTS

Supporting Documents

Why nonfiction prompts?

Giving students reasons to write across the curriculum is one of the most powerful and time-saving strategies in the educator's toolkit. The content areas present numerous opportunities for students to engage in writing for authentic purposes; in turn, writing is an excellent vehicle for students to demonstrate their understandings of the essential concepts being taught in a content area. These prompts have been written for teachers who are committed to standards-based instruction and to integrating their curriculum. They were selected to complement (History/Social Studies/Science/Math) units of study and to give students practice in all four domains of writing.

How do I use them?

Teachers may choose to use the prompts in a variety of ways:

- As *writing-process* assignments, wherein students have several weeks to synthesize and apply essential understandings of new concepts to a quality piece of writing.

- For teacher-guided *interactive writing* lessons, during which teachers can reinforce content-area learning while also assisting students to refine their writing techniques.

- As *performance assessments,* wherein students demonstrate they can effectively answer essential questions generated from a unit of study in a content area.

- In some cases, as a *quick-write pretest* to assess students' preexisting knowledge before commencement of a unit.

When not to use them

Although some prompts could be given as quick-write assessments of students' preexisting knowledge, these prompts should be given primarily during or upon completion of a unit of study. They are not designed to be given "cold" as a test instrument to assess student writing proficiency. Clearly, if these prompts are given prior to instruction, students' writing scores will potentially be undermined by their inability to support their ideas with relevant facts and details.

Why is the wording so sophisticated?

You will note that the wording used in the prompts often mirrors that found in the standards themselves. Such terminology will be intimidating to students only if there are no strong learning associations with the meaning of the words. Kindergartners have no problems remembering what a *Tyrannosaurus rex* is; with sound instruction, nor do they have difficulty understanding terms such as *evaporation.*

Some prompts don't exactly fit the content I taught

These prompts are suggestions and a place to start. Teachers are encouraged to modify the wording of these prompts, or write their own prompts, to better fit the emphasis of the unit and the purpose of the writing. For example, they may wish to vary the number of paragraphs required, depending on what part of the year the unit was completed. They may feel that students would do better responding to the prompt in the form of a poem or a letter rather than a straight composition. Keep two important things in mind, however: students need practice in all four domains of writing, and the content taught must be standards-based.

What should I consider when writing my own prompts or when modifying existing prompts?

The wording of a prompt can either motivate or intimidate a writer. Good prompts make it very clear to students what you are asking of them. Compare the following two prompts:

1. *Explain precipitation and evaporation in at least two paragraphs.*

2. *Your friend doesn't know how there is always enough water stored in the sky to fall as rain. She also doesn't know how puddles on the playground can just disappear after a while. Write a report of at least two paragraphs to help your friend understand precipitation and evaporation.*

Prompts like the first one tend to reinforce a student's notion that writing is what one does to pass a test or complete an assignment for a grade. By contrast, the second prompt takes the following points into consideration:

- The audience for whom the student is writing is clear (a friend).

- The purpose of the writing has been specified (to help the friend understand).

- The type of writing required is referred to as a "report," reminding students that this piece of writing should be presented as straightforward prose and will not be, for example, in a letter, poem, or story format.

- The minimum number of paragraphs/sentences required has been specified.

- Some clues have been put into the prompt by way of the scenario to assist students in activating their existing knowledge on the subject.

Some other things to consider when writing prompts:

- If you are creating the prompt specifically to assess student knowledge about a content area at the end of a unit of study, design the prompt around the essential question(s) you began with at the start of the unit.

- Don't ask students to talk about anything personal that may be seen as an invasion of privacy.

- Avoid asking students to write specifically about holidays (e.g., Halloween, Christmas) or birthdays. These can be sensitive areas for some students and their parents because of religious beliefs or negative feelings about holidays.

- Be sure you could effectively write to the prompt yourself. Plan out what you would do, as an expert writer, to satisfy the requirements of the prompt.

- Write prompts that will give students practice in all four domains of writing.

What are the four domains of writing students need to practice, and why is it important for teachers to know what they are?

We use the *sensory/descriptive* domain when we write down our deepest feelings in a diary or use our five senses to describe an unusual sea creature for a scientific journal. We enjoy *imaginative/narrative* writing every time we read a novel, watch a television drama, or catch a movie. When we fill out forms, make to-do lists, summarize documents, or write directions, we are using the *practical/informative* domain. We dive into the *analytical/expository* domain when we write a campaign speech, justify an opinion, or e-mail friends convincing them to go to the holiday destination of our choosing.

The majority of writing we do in life falls under the *practical/informative* and *analytical/ expository* domains—but at times those domains will contain elements of the other two. For example, a report on the results of an experiment will be more effective if it contains good sensory description; a historical novel can be a source of practical information while also being an imaginative narrative. Hence, it is vital for students to receive instruction and practice in *all four* domains. Moreover, it is crucial for students and teachers to know that although a piece may contain several elements spanning more than one domain, ultimately it is categorized by its *primary* objective. The following table gives definitions and examples of each domain.

The Domain	Its Primary Objective	Some Examples
Sensory/Descriptive	To describe an object, a moment in time, or feelings experienced in vivid, sensory detail.	• Detailed recordings of observations made of a fossil • A poem describing feelings experienced after suffering an injustice • A character sketch of Abraham Lincoln
Imaginative/Narrative	To tell what happened in a logical sequence. This could be a real-life or imaginary series of events.	• The autobiography of Thomas Edison • The story of Charlie Crawley, who started out as a caterpillar and ended up as a butterfly • A comic strip portraying Newton's discovery of gravity
Practical/Informative	To present basic information with clarity.	• A business letter to the supplier of the canteen milk cartons informing them of leaks • Step-by step instructions for performing an experiment • A summary of a *National Geographic* article
Analytical/Expository	To explain, analyze, compare and contrast, or persuade.	• A television commercial persuading viewers to recycle their soda cans • An explanation of the impact of the Gold Rush on life choices made by Chinese immigrants • A comparison of sedimentary and igneous rocks

What kind of scoring guide should I use to evaluate proficiency?

Whatever scoring guide or rubric you decide to use, ensure that the *students* know the criteria being used to assess proficiency. Those criteria may be embodied in an existing scoring guide or one you and the students have created together around the demands of a specific prompt.

Decide what you are *primarily* evaluating. Are you mainly trying to determine whether students have internalized information and acquired essential understandings, or are you evaluating *how well* they are able to use language to express what they know? Ultimately, of course, your objective is to develop proficiency in both. Certainly, if a prompt were given as a writing-process assignment to be completed over several weeks, you should reasonably expect *both* excellent content and excellent written expression to be evident. If, however, the prompt is given as a posttest at the conclusion of a unit, you may choose not to heavily penalize mistakes in sentence structure and conventions, as long as students demonstrate essential understanding(s) of the content. If you are more concerned with a student's ability to state and justify an opinion in a quick-write assignment, you may choose on that occasion not to heavily penalize inaccurate information.

The following are samples of an analytic scoring guide and a holistic scoring guide. An *analytic scoring* guide allows you to assess a student's writing proficiency trait by trait. Simply give a 1, 2, 3, or 4 score for each trait; a "3" score indicates proficiency in that area. An analytic scoring guide enables teachers to focus their instruction on those areas of writing in which a student is not yet proficient. In other words, the assessment informs instruction. The *holistic scoring guide,* in contrast, is less specific and gives the student a score based on the teacher's overall impression of the piece. As with the analytic scoring guide, a "3" is considered a proficient score.

Middle and Secondary Analytic Scoring Guide

TRAIT	4 **Exceeds Grade-Level Expectations**	3 **Proficient**	2 **Approaching Proficiency**	1 **Not Proficient**
Essential understandings of content	Clearly demonstrates essential understanding(s). Provides strong, credible support of the topic and shares insights that go beyond the obvious and predictable. Maintains a consistent point of view.	Demonstrates essential understanding(s). Supporting details and ideas may at times be too general or out of balance with the main idea. Maintains a mostly consistent point of view.	An attempt was made to address the main idea, but the essential understanding(s) are not clear. Attempts are made to support ideas, but may be irrelevant. Inconsistent point of view.	Ideas are unclear and lack a central link to essential understanding(s).

Middle and Secondary Analytic Scoring Guide *(Continued)*

TRAIT	4 Exceeds Grade-Level Expectations	3 Proficient	2 Approaching Proficiency	1 Not Proficient
Organization	Uses an organizational structure that fits the purpose of the writing task. Constructs inviting introductions and satisfying conclusions. Selects effective transitions and employs purposeful pacing.	Uses an organizational structure that fits the purpose of the writing task. Creates clear introductions and conclusions. Transitions are adequate, but pacing may be inconsistent.	Uses an organizational structure that addresses only parts of the writing task. Has undeveloped beginnings and/or conclusions and weak or overused transitions. Little knowledge of pacing.	Uses an organizational structure that may be haphazard and disjointed. Has weak beginning and conclusion.

Middle and Secondary Analytic Scoring Guide *(Continued)*

TRAIT	4 Exceeds Grade-Level Expectations	3 Proficient	2 Approaching Proficiency	1 Not Proficient
Content Vocabulary	Demonstrates understanding of vocabulary related to content. Uses words in an interesting, precise, and natural way. Uses fresh and lively expressions that at times include figurative language or slang.	Demonstrates understanding of vocabulary related to content. Uses words in a precise and natural way appropriate to audience and purpose.	Attempts to use content vocabulary words, but does not apply them appropriately. Words used are generally imprecise and at times may not be appropriate to audience and purpose.	Words are limited, monotonous, or misused. Only the most general kind of message is communicated.

Middle and Secondary Analytic Scoring Guide (Continued)

TRAIT	4 Exceeds Grade-Level Expectations	3 Proficient	2 Approaching Proficiency	1 Not Proficient
Voice	Demonstrates strong audience awareness and creates a strong interaction with the reader. There is a strong sense of commitment to the topic. An appropriate voice or tone is consistently employed. Topic is brought to life through conviction, excitement, or humor.	Demonstrates audience awareness; there is a sense of commitment to the topic most of the time.	Demonstrates limited audience awareness; the sense of commitment to the topic is inconsistent. Uses a voice that is overly informal or impersonal and flat.	Shows no audience awareness. It is hard to sense the person and purpose behind the words. Voice is consistently flat.

TRAIT	4 Exceeds Grade-Level Expectations	3 Proficient	2 Approaching Proficiency	1 Not Proficient
Sentence fluency	Sentences are well constructed with correct word order and subject/verb agreement; there are no run-ons or fragments. Employs correct tenses and uses pronouns correctly. Varies sentence structure, length, and beginnings to strengthen the meaning of the text and draw attention to the main ideas.	Uses complete sentences. Occasional errors in word order, tense, pronoun usage, subject/verb agreement, or use of run-ons and fragments do not detract from meaning. Varies sentence length and beginnings.	Errors in word order, pronoun usage, tense, subject/verb agreement, and/or use of run-ons and fragments detract from meaning. The sentence structure tends to be mechanical rather than fluid.	Errors in sentence structure obscure meaning and often cause the reader to slow down or reread.

Middle and Secondary Analytic Scoring Guide *(Continued)*

TRAIT	4 **Exceeds Grade-Level Expectations**	3 **Proficient**	2 **Approaching Proficiency**	1 **Not Proficient**
Conventions	Strong control of standard writing conventions. Little editing is needed. Uses correct grammar and usage to enhance communication and contribute to clarity and style. Consistently uses paragraph breaks that reinforce organization and meaning.	Reasonable control of standard writing conventions. Occasional errors in capitalization, punctuation, and spelling do not interfere with readability. Grammar and usage guide the reader through the text. Employs paragraph breaks that reinforce organization and meaning.	Makes frequent capitalization, punctuation, and/or spelling errors that distract the reader. Errors in grammar and usage interfere with readability and meaning. Paragraph breaks may not effectively contribute to organization and meaning.	Shows little control of standard writing conventions. Errors in grammar and usage block the meaning of the writing, making it difficult to focus on the message.

Student Name: _____ Date: _____

Middle and Secondary Holistic Scoring Guide

4—Exceeds Grade-Level Expectations

- Demonstrates essential understanding(s) about the content and gives supporting details that go beyond the predictable. Maintains a consistent point of view.

- Uses an organizational structure that fits the purpose of the writing task. Constructs inviting introductions and satisfying conclusions. Consistently uses paragraph breaks that reinforce organization and meaning. Uses effective transitions and pacing that move the reader easily through the text.

- Demonstrates understanding of vocabulary related to content. Uses fresh and lively expressions that at times include figurative language or slang.

- Demonstrates strong audience awareness; there is a sense of a person and a purpose behind the words. Consistently employs an appropriate voice or tone. Brings topic to life through conviction, excitement, or humor; there is a strong interaction with the reader.

- Demonstrates stylistic control. The sentence structure strengthens the meaning of the text and draws attention to key ideas. Correct grammar and usage contribute to clarity and style. Little editing is needed.

3—Proficient

- Demonstrates essential understanding(s) about the content. Supporting details and ideas may at times be too general or out of balance with the main idea, but maintains a consistent point of view.

- Uses an organizational structure that fits the purpose of the writing task. Creates clear introductions and conclusions. Employs paragraph breaks that generally reinforce organization and meaning. Uses adequate transitions. Pacing may be inconsistent.

- Demonstrates understanding of vocabulary related to content. Uses words in an interesting, precise, and natural way appropriate to audience and purpose.

- Demonstrates audience awareness; there is a sense of a person and purpose behind the words. Employs an appropriate voice or tone most of the time.

- Demonstrates reasonable control of standard writing conventions. Some syntax, spelling, capitalization, and punctuation errors occur, but do not interfere with meaning.

2—Approaching Proficiency

- Attempts to address the main idea, but does *not* demonstrate essential understanding(s) about the content.

- Made an attempt to organize the text, but the overall structure may be inconsistent or not appropriate for the writing task. May use an introduction or conclusion. Sequence of ideas may not be effectively presented.

- Attempts to use content vocabulary words, but does not apply them appropriately. Words used are generally imprecise and at times may not be appropriate to audience and purpose.

- Demonstrates limited audience awareness; there is little sense of a person and purpose behind the words. Uses a voice that is overly informal or impersonal and flat. There is little sense of "writing to be read."

- Demonstrates limited control of standard conventions. The sentence structure may be mechanical rather than fluid. Frequent errors in syntax, spelling, capitalization, and punctuation detract from meaning.

1—Not Proficient

- Ideas are unclear and lack a central link to essential understanding(s).

- Organizational structure is not appropriate for the purpose. Weak beginning and/or conclusion. No logical sequence of ideas.

- Words are limited, monotonous, and/or misused. Only the most general kind of message is communicated.

- Shows no audience awareness; it is hard to sense a person and purpose behind the words.

- Little control of standard conventions. Errors in syntax, spelling, capitalization, and punctuation obscure meaning, making it difficult for the reader to focus on the message.

How can I help students evaluate and improve their own writing performance?

Receiving specific feedback from teachers, especially during a one-to-one conference, is critical for improving student writing. It is equally important to give students opportunities to confer with each other. Students soon find out how well they are communicating their knowledge in a piece of writing when fellow students tell them some portion of it doesn't make sense. Additionally, the process of evaluating the writing of others helps the students doing the evaluating to focus attention on their own strengths and weaknesses. The deliberate acts of thinking about, and evaluating, our own learning and learning processes is known as metacognition. Encouraging this kind of self-reflection in students is crucial if we want them to become independent learners and effective communicators. Peer conferencing allows students to explain what they learned and how they learned it, which not only helps to anchor new concepts in memory, but also provides the foundation and scaffolding on which to build further learning. This sharing of knowledge, ideas, and processes has the added benefit of contributing positively to overall class performance.

When asking a student to evaluate another student's writing, it is essential, first, to define the criteria by which the piece is to be judged, and second, to establish some conferencing guidelines. If this is not done, the feedback may be either too vague or too brutal to be constructive. The following "house rules" are worth modeling, discussing, and even posting for the class:

1. I will read the piece through, using stick-on notes or flags to mark those areas I want to discuss with the author afterward.

2. I will give careful thought to the written evaluation I complete so that my colleague will know in which areas proficiency has or has not been achieved.

3. I will not make any marks or corrections on the piece itself. Any changes I suggest will be made by the author's hand only, after the author has accepted them.

4. I will back up my praise or concerns about the writing with evidence from the piece.

5. I will help the author to understand how to communicate essential concepts more effectively.

Peer Evaluation and Conferencing Form

Title of Piece: _____ Written by: _____

Evaluator: _____ Date: _____

Facet of Writing	The piece is proficient in this area, as evidenced by...	The piece is not yet proficient in this area, as evidenced by...
Content Demonstrates understanding of the essential concepts needed to write to the prompt. Gives supporting details that help get the point across. Maintains a consistent point of view.		

Facet of Writing	The piece is proficient in this area, as evidenced by...	The piece is not yet proficient in this area, as evidenced by...
Organization Uses an organizational structure that fits the purpose of the writing task. Creates clear introductions and conclusions. Transitions are adequate and the pacing is consistent.		
Content Vocabulary Demonstrates understanding of vocabulary words related to the subject. Uses these and other words in a precise and natural way appropriate to the audience and purpose.		

Facet of Writing	The piece is proficient in this area, as evidenced by...	The piece is not yet proficient in this area, as evidenced by...
Voice Demonstrates audience awareness; there is a sense of commitment to the topic.		
Sentence Fluency Uses complete sentences and varies sentence structure, length, and beginnings.		

Facet of Writing	The piece is proficient in this area, as evidenced by...	The piece is not yet proficient in this area, as evidenced by...
Conventions Grammar and usage guide the reader through the text. Employs paragraph breaks that reinforce organization and meaning. Spelling, capitalization, and punctuation are mostly correct.		

The middle ground, where both reason and research are found, is that while demographic factors such as poverty and second languages are clearly associated with lower student performance, the impact of these factors is less than the impact of great teaching and school leadership.

—Douglas B. Reeves, Ph.D. (2004, p. 170)

   H_2O

Is it warmer or cooler near large bodies of water? Explain the relationship between the oceans and climate.

H_2O

Although they have important roles to play in adolescents' literacy development, language arts and reading teachers need content-area teachers to show students how to read and write like a scientist, historian, or mathematician.

—Richard Vacca (2002, p. 10)

  H₂O

Describe the four components of Earth's system: geosphere, hydrosphere, atmosphere, and biosphere. Include an illustration of the planet Earth and label the specific areas. Draw and label a stick figure of yourself in the area where you live.

Content literacy is often defined as the level of reading and writing skill that learners need in an academic subject to comprehend and respond to ideas in text used for instructional purposes.

—Richard Vacca (2002, p. 7)

  H₂O

Newscasters usually call them "natural catastrophes." Explain how you would demonstrate "destructive forces" on land forms to your classmates. Include illustrations for "before" and "after" conditions.

H_2O

An effective accountability system must answer at least four common sense questions: one about individual student achievement; a second about school performance; a third about ways to help students learn; and a fourth about determining educational effectiveness.

—Douglas B. Reeves, Ph.D. (2004, p. 26)

H_2O

A worm helps make soil. People do, too. Define what "soil" consists of and how it is made over time.

      H₂O

The persons responsible for the education of our children must have a clear idea of what they must do to help all students achieve.

—Douglas B. Reeves, Ph.D. (2004, p. 96)

  H_2O

How do global patterns of atmospheric movement influence your local weather? Explain where your local weather comes from and why.

H_2O

Only with a written response from students can teachers create the strategies necessary to improve performance for both teacher and learner.

—Douglas B. Reeves, Ph.D. (2004, p. 190)

H_2O

Water is essential to life! Describe the water cycle and how human beings have affected it. Use a diagram with captions.

H_2O

Effective accountability systems . . . are "done-for" teachers and students: to enhance their interaction and improve student learning.

—Douglas B. Reeves, Ph.D. (2004, p. 49)

H₂O

What causes an earthquake to happen? What are aftershocks? Describe what happens to lithospheric plates when they move and cause an earthquake.

*Achievement comes from a focus on clear standards,
not from the inappropriate complacency that results
from short-term victories over classmates.*

—Douglas B. Reeves, Ph.D. (2004, p. 37)

H₂O

Sailing is fun but requires knowledge in order to keep safe. For example, you would need to understand high and low tides. Explain the relationship between gravity and tides.

H_2O

SCIENCE   EARTH SCIENCE

ANALYTICAL/EXPOSITORY

The word "strategy" often connotes lofty vision and grand plans; in fact, it is simply a method of achieving a result.

—Douglas B. Reeves, Ph.D. (2004, p. 16)

 H₂O

Was land once under an ocean? Was the climate once hot and humid where it is now dry and cold? Describe how a fossil provides evidence of how life and environmental conditions have changed over time.

H_2O

The central focus of a standards-based system is the achievement of standards by as many students as possible.

—Douglas B. Reeves, Ph.D. (2004, p. 180)

H₂O

Name several objects in your environment. Explain how you estimate size and/or distance of those objects.

[A]ccountability information can offer teachers and school leaders insights into effective practices to improve student achievement.

—Douglas B. Reeves, Ph.D. (2004, p. 170)

Cemeteries are fascinating places to gather data.
Some of the tombstones are glossy and clear;
others are pitted and worn. Explain how living
organisms affect the composition of the atmosphere
and contribute to the weathering of stone statues.

      H₂O

Good writing, regardless of the mode of discourse, causes writers to think. That thinking involves a productive dialectic between analysis and synthesis.

—Tom Romano (1995, p. 6)

     H_2O

Using a concept map, explain what you know about our major source of energy, the sun.

Teacher assessment gives a more comprehensive view of student performance than a single test score.

—Douglas B. Reeves, Ph.D. (2004, p. 55)

H₂O

You want to go hiking with friends on the weekend. It has rained heavily for the past week. Explain how you would determine the probability of rain for the weekend.

H_2O

Student writers need a standard to work toward. In a class in which students evaluate themselves, evaluative modules provide a standard of quality.

—Natalia Perchemlides and Carolyn Coutant (2004, p. 55)

 H₂O

The moon is a natural satellite of our planet, Earth. Describe the regular and predictable motion of the moon.

   H₂O

Good teachers realize that a major part of teaching is helping kids understand themselves as learners and helping them begin to think like professionals in whatever discipline they are studying.

—Marcia D'Arcangelo (2002, p. 12)

H_2O

Develop a concept map to identify a well-known scientist or engineer and how he or she has contributed to science and society.

H_2O

*The effective use of accountability data requires
the commonplace use of research, assessment, and
communication by teachers and school leaders.*

—Douglas B. Reeves, Ph.D. (2004, p. 175)

 H₂O

Science is always evolving—what does this mean? Summarize a scientific, engineering, or technological discovery that changed the way people communicate.

 H_2O

Helping writers develop fluency and competence in a variety of technologies is a key part of teaching writing in this century.

—Kathleen Blake Yancey (2004, p. 38)

H_2O

Think about a time when you and another person interpreted the same data differently. Explain why data can have more than one explanation. Use an example from an investigation.

When students are knee-deep in the process of composing,
they need feedback from both teachers and peers.

—Natalia Perchemlides and Carolyn Coutant (2004, p. 54)

H₂O

Harvard Medical School, the National Geographic Society, and NASA communicate their research data with other institutions around the world. Explain why it is important to repeat data-collection procedures and to share data among groups.

       H_2O

Without the writer's mindful involvement, the writing process is like a ship without a rudder—in motion, but out of control.

—Bruce Saddler and Heidi Andrade (2004, p. 48)

H_2O

Write a definition of the term *species.* Explain how one species you are familiar with interacts with its environment, population, and community of other species.

H₂O

*Clear, accessible instructional rubrics can give students
repeated practice with planning, revising, and editing.*

—Bruce Saddler and Heidi Andrade (2004, p. 51)

H₂O

Describe your understanding of nutrition and energy flow. Use specific examples for plants and animals.

In response to the diverse needs of its students, a school district must be committed to maintaining equity and must set high standards and expectations for all students.

—Douglas B. Reeves, Ph.D. (2004, p. 94)

 H₂O

Explain your understanding of how a single-celled organism sustains life. How does it gain energy? Reproduce? Put your thoughts in comic-strip format.

H2O

For subject teachers to implement principles and practices of secondary reading and writing[,] they must first recognize reading and writing as meaning-making processes that can support their instructional goals, particularly those related to understanding content.

—Vicki Jacobs (2002, p. 61)

H₂O

Explain the various systems within the human body
and how they interact.

        H₂O

Effective assessment is the foundation of effective accountability.

—Douglas B. Reeves, Ph.D. (2004, p. 17)

H₂O

Think of your favorite flower. Describe how this flowering plant reproduces. Illustrate the structures and process.

H_2O

In order to provide useful information about student achievement, an accountability system must be based on clear standards that have been communicated to students, parents, teachers, and other district stakeholders.

—Douglas B. Reeves, Ph.D. (2004, p. 26)

H₂O

You are a unique person. Write about yourself in a scientific way. Explain *heredity* and give examples of inherited, as well as learned, traits.

Students should never have to wander aimlessly through their educational journeys, wondering what they need to do in order to please the teacher.

—Douglas B. Reeves, Ph.D. (2004, p. 33)

  H$_2$O

Define the terms *producers*, *consumers*, and *decomposers* as part of an ecosystem. Give examples of each. Identify your role in this system.

     H₂O

All teachers in all subjects share the responsibility for literacy development in middle and high school.

—Richard Vacca (2002, p. 10)

H_2O

What factors determine the number of organisms supported by an ecosystem? Explain the factors for plants and animals.

Students need frequent feedback about their performances as compared with clear, objective standards—not as compared with the performance of their peers.

—Douglas B. Reeves, Ph.D. (2004, p. 38)

Explain why an extinction of a species occurs. Use an example you have read or heard about. Summarize what happened to the plant or animal and why.

H_2O

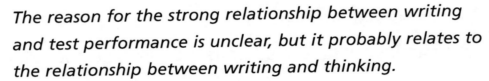

The reason for the strong relationship between writing and test performance is unclear, but it probably relates to the relationship between writing and thinking.

—Douglas B. Reeves, Ph.D. (2002, p. 5)

H₂O

NONFICTION WRITING FOR SCIENCE

You have discovered a new organism. Illustrate how it looks, moves, and obtains food. Write about where it lives and how its characteristics adapted to the environment.

H₂O

The purpose of accountability is to improve student achievement.

—Douglas B. Reeves, Ph.D. (2004, p. 41)

  H_2O

An unknown substance is left on your lab tray. You are not sure whether it is toxic. How would you handle it? Explain how you determine the characteristic properties of the substance in order to identify it.

H_2O

Fairness and accountability are not about "beating" someone else, but they are certainly about winning the battle against inequity, injustice, and ignorance.

—Douglas B. Reeves, Ph.D. (2004, p. 100)

  H₂O

Explain the relationship between elements, compounds, and mixtures. Give at least one example of each.

H₂O

Accountability systems that fail to recognize the importance of teaching . . . will fail to achieve their primary objective: the improvement of student learning.

—Douglas B. Reeves, Ph.D. (2004, p. 58)

H₂O

Describe different ways electrical energy is transferred when heat, sound, and light are produced. Use examples from your everyday life.

H_2O

For learning, the act of writing provides a chronology of our thoughts, which we can then label, objectify, modify, or build on[,] and it engages us in becoming invested in our ideas and learning. Writing-to-learn forms and extends thinking and thus deepens understanding. . . . Like reading-to-learn, it is a meaning-making process.

—Vicki Jacobs (2002, p. 60)

90

 H₂O

Explain your strategies for demonstrating the position, direction of motion, and speed of two rolling objects—both are the same size, texture, and shape, but one has twice as much mass. Create a graph of supporting evidence.

H_2O

The principles and practices of secondary reading and writing provide means by which students can move from understanding to demonstrating understanding.

—Vicki Jacobs (2002, p. 61)

H_2O

You are an astronaut. Explain what happens when two identical objects are "tossed up": one on Earth and the other on a space station orbiting the Earth. What forces are acting on each object and what are the results?

H₂O

Writing helps students think about the content, reflect on their knowledge of the content, and share their thoughts with the teacher.

—Douglas Fisher, Nancy Frey, and Douglas Williams (2002, p. 72)

H_2O

The hazards of cooking: Explain why and how heat moves from a boiling liquid to a metal spoon placed into the liquid.

Teachers can develop reflective critics within their classrooms by teaching students how to use rubrics to assess their own and their classmates' writing. Student assessment has the additional advantage of promoting self-regulation because it gives students some of the responsibility for judging written work instead of placing that responsibility solely on the teacher.

—Bruce Saddler and Heidi Andrade (2004, p. 51)

H_2O

Define *unbalanced forces*. Describe a situation that demonstrates your definition clearly.

      H₂O

As a matter of fairness and good educational practice, students deserve to have their work evaluated against an objective standard.

—Douglas B. Reeves, Ph.D. (2004, p. 34)

 H₂O

NONFICTION WRITING FOR SCIENCE

Explain how the human eye "sees" an object. Then create a diagram clearly labeling all parts of the eye.

H_2O

Writing should involve discovering, analyzing, synthesizing and evaluating—not just copying and downloading.

—Michael M. Yell (2002, p. 66)

  H₂O

The sun emits light energy, a small amount of which is transferred to Earth. Where does this energy go next? Explain, using at least two examples from your everyday life.

      H_2O

SCIENCE—PHYSICAL SCIENCE

Writing, in this instance, is a particularly powerful tool for helping adolescents listen, reflect, converse with themselves, and tackle both cultural messages and peer pressures.

—Peter Elbow (2004, p. 12)

 H₂O

NONFICTION WRITING FOR SCIENCE

How can the most accurate monthly observations
of rainfall in the school parking lot be collected?
Explain how you would do this.

When teachers embed writing strategies in instruction, they enrich and enliven the required curriculum.

—Michael M. Yell (2002, p. 66)

H₂O

NONFICTION WRITING FOR SCIENCE

How does a light microscope enhance the study of a microorganism? What additional information does this technological tool provide?

H2O

Writing for social action is an ideal way to energize students, especially students who see school as pointless and dull.

—Randy Boomer (2004, p. 34)

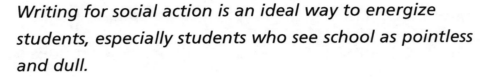

H₂O

What are the pros and cons of using a map as a model of a specific area of the Earth?

H_2O

When we give students freedom to take risks, a stake in their own progress and the language to understand the writing process, their fear of writing will turn to true excitement.

—Natalia Perchemlides and Carolyn Coutant (2004, p. 56)

What tools would you use to gather, analyze,
and interpret data for a stream water quality study?
How would you use them? Why?

      H_2O

Researchers helped us struggling teachers see that when students actually immersed themselves in the business of writing, they learned how to tackle ideas, play with language, and create structures that expressed their thoughts.

—Cathy Fleischer (2004, p. 25)

   H_2O

Describe how mathematics is used to ask and answer questions about the natural world. What mathematical functions or concepts have you used in science class?

      H_2O

Inquiry treats writing as a problem-solving activity in which students come to understand something that they want to say before they begin drafting.

—Vicki Jacobs (2002, p. 60)

H_2O

Explain what measurement system is used in scientific investigations. Why is it used? What measurement units are used to record mass, volume, and length?

Reading, writing, and content learning are related.

—Douglas Fisher, Nancy Frey, and Douglas Williams (2002, p. 70)

  H_2O

Describe various ways in which scientific data can be displayed as evidence to fellow scientists.

H_2O

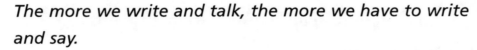

The more we write and talk, the more we have to write and say.

—Peter Elbow (2004, p. 13)

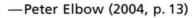

H₂O

Identify some of your own questions that can be answered by scientific inquiry and explain why.

Students who write with confidence will be more open to strategies that allow them to express their written voice.

—Tom Romano (2004, p. 20)

H₂O

NONFICTION WRITING FOR SCIENCE

Science fair time is coming! How should evidence be organized to present the strongest explanation?

H₂O

Learning to write means learning to speak out, to make one's voice heard in the great human conversation. And by teaching students to raise their voices through writing on social issues that concern them, we teach them to participate actively in a democracy.

—Randy Boomer (2004, p. 34)

H_2O

There is talk of introducing eagles to your area.
First, a current report of birds living in the area
is commissioned. Design a scientific investigation
students could conduct to identify the birds
common to your area.

      H₂O

Great teachers know only too well that writing is hard work—exhausting for students and massively time consuming for teachers. But they also understand that if students are to make knowledge their own, they must wrestle with facts, struggle with details, and rework raw information into language that reaches an audience.

—Laurel Schmidt (2004, p. 45)

Explain how you would track animals that live in your neighborhood so you can discover the diversity of wildlife present.

      H_2O 123

*Peer assessment helps students reflect on their own writing,
recognize dissonances, and create solutions.*

—Natalie Perchemlides and Carolyn Coutant (2004, p. 55)

  H₂O

Obesity is a national health issue! Design a solution or product that helps middle school students to exercise daily for good health.

H₂O

SCIENCE — SCIENCE IN SOCIETY

Citizens have influence only to the extent that they use it, and writing transforms an important but silent idea into a powerful source of influence.

—Douglas B. Reeves, Ph.D. (2002, p. 5)

  H_2O

Explain the pros and cons of alcohol use by teenagers.

H₂O

Bibliography

Boomer, R. "Speaking Out for Social Action." *Educational Leadership* 62, no. 2 (October 2004): 34–37.

D'Arcangelo, M. "The Challenge of Content-Area Reading: A Conversation with Donna Ogle." *Educational Leadership* 60, no. 3 (November 2002): 12–15.

Elbow, P. "Writing First." *Educational Leadership* 62, no. 2 (October 2004): 8–13.

Fisher, D., N. Frey, and D. Williams. "Seven Literacy Strategies that Work." *Educational Leadership* 60, no. 3 (November 2002): 70–73.

Fleischer, C. "Professional Development for Teacher-Writers." *Educational Leadership* 62, no. 2 (October 2004): 24–28.

Jacobs, V. "Reading, Writing, and Understanding." *Educational Leadership* 60, no. 3 (November 2002): 58–61.

Perchemlides, N., and C. Coutant. "Growing Beyond Grades." *Educational Leadership* 62, no. 2 (October 2004): 53–56.

Reeves, D. B. *Accountability in Action.* Englewood, CO: Advanced Learning Press, 2004.

Reeves, D. B. *Reason to Write* (Elementary school edition). New York: Kaplan Publishing, 2002.

Romano, T. "The Power of Voice." *Educational Leadership* 62, no. 2 (October 2004): 20–23.

Romano, T. *Writing with Passion: Life Stories, Multiple Genres.* Portsmouth, NH: Heinemann, 1995.

Saddler, B., and H. Andrade. "The Writing Rubric." *Educational Leadership* 62, no. 2 (October 2004): 48–52.

Schmidt, L. "Is There a Hemingway in the House?" *Educational Leadership* 62, no. 2 (October 2004): 42–45.

Vacca, R. "From Efficient Decoders to Strategic Readers." *Educational Leadership* 60, no. 3 (November 2002): 6–11.

Yancey, K. B. "Using Multiple Technologies to Teach Writing." *Educational Leadership* 62, no. 2 (October 2004): 38–40.

Yell, M. "Putting Gel Pen to Paper." *Educational Leadership* 60, no. 3 (November 2002): 63–66.